101 EASY-TO-READ SHORT STORIES
© J.J Santaella 2023 All Rights Reserved
Kindle Direct Publishing

Paperback Edition 2023

Dedicated with much love to:

This book was made with a lot of love for you. I hope you like it and have fun. Enjoy it!

101
EASY-TO-READ
SHORT STORIES

A day at the beach

Long ago, I used to go to the beach with my family. I liked to feel the sea breeze on my face and the soft sand under my feet.

I remember one particular day when we went to the beach very early. We arrived before the sun came up and found a quiet spot to sit.

My daughter and my grandson were with me, and I remember how my grandson played with a bucket and shovel in the sand. I watched him as he built a beautiful sandcastle, and I loved seeing his creativity.

Later, my daughter and I went into the water. The sea was cold at first, but soon I got used to it and began to enjoy the feeling of the salty water on my skin. We laughed a lot and played in the water like we were girls again.

Afterwards, we sat on the towel and ate some snacks we had brought. The sun was hot and we felt the heat on our skin, but it was okay because the sea breeze kept us cool.

It was a very peaceful and happy day, and I remember it fondly. Now, even though I can't go to the beach anymore, I close my eyes and can feel the sun and sea breeze again.

The end.

A mi grandmother's birthday

A few years ago, my grandmother turned 80 and her family decided to throw her a big birthday party. We were all very excited to celebrate with her and make her feel special.

We prepared everything in advance: we decorated the house with balloons and streamers, bought a big birthday cake, and prepared a delicious meal. In addition, we invited the whole family, her friends, and some people from the community who knew and loved my grandmother very much.

On the day of the party, my grandmother was radiant. She was dressed in her best clothes and wore a big flower hat. Everyone gave her presents and wished her a happy birthday. She was so happy to be surrounded by so many loved ones.

After eating, we sang "Happy Birthday" and my grandmother blew out the candles on her cake. Then we sat down to chat and remember happy moments we had shared with her. My grandmother laughed and smiled, and told us how much she appreciated that everyone had come to celebrate with her.

It was a very beautiful and emotional party, and I will never forget it. Every time I think about that day, I feel happy and grateful to have been able to share it with my grandmother.

THE END.

A pet store

A few days ago, I went to a pet store with my niece. She wanted to buy a goldfish, and I decided to accompany her. When we arrived at the store, a very friendly salesperson greeted us and showed us all the animals they had.

There were many interesting animals: rabbits, hamsters, parakeets, and cats. But my niece only wanted a goldfish. Finally, we found one that she really liked and bought it.

While the salesperson prepared the fish in a bag for us to take home, I observed the other animals. A white and gray cat looked at me with its big, round eyes, and I thought it was very cute. I wondered if someone would adopt it soon.

When we got home with the fish, my niece put it in its fish tank and watched it swim. I was happy to have accompanied her to the pet store and to have seen so many cute animals. I even thought about adopting the white and gray cat, but decided to ask my family first.

Sometimes, it's good to visit a pet store and see the animals. They make you feel good and remind you how beautiful nature is.

THE END.

My Uncle's Farm.

My uncle has a beautiful farm. He lives there surrounded by many animals and crops. I visited his farm a few days ago and I found everything I saw very interesting.

On my uncle's farm, there are many animals such as horses, cows, pigs, chickens, and ducks. He also has a very affectionate dog that is always ready to play. I had a lot of fun feeding the chickens and watching the horses run through the fields.

In addition to the animals, my uncle grows many fruits and vegetables. He has apple trees, tomatoes, carrots, lettuces, and many other plants that grow beautifully on his farm. I loved eating an apple freshly picked from the tree, it was delicious.

He also showed me how to work on a farm. He showed me the tools he uses to work the land and explained to me how to take care of the animals. It is a very hard job, but very rewarding.

I really enjoyed my visit to my uncle's farm. It was a very special day where I learned a lot about nature and working in the countryside. I would like to come back someday and see how everything has grown.

The Picnic in the Park

Last weekend, my family and I went for a picnic in the park. It was a very beautiful and sunny day. We brought a large blanket to sit on the grass and a basket full of delicious food.

We ate ham and cheese sandwiches, fresh fruits like apples and grapes, and sweet cookies. We also brought orange juice and water to drink.

While we were eating, we saw children running and playing in the park. There was a swing, a slide, and a playground area with many fun toys. I was very happy to see them play, it reminded me of my own children when they were little.

After eating, we walked around the park a bit. We saw many beautiful trees and flowers. We also saw a pond with ducks swimming. It was very relaxing and nice to be surrounded by nature.

We ended our picnic day in the park watching the sunset. The clouds were painted with red, orange, and pink tones. It was a beautiful show that made us feel very happy and grateful.

The picnic in the park was a very special day full of joy. I would like to go back someday and do the same with my friends and family.

The Concert in the Park

The other day, my friend and I went to a concert in the park. The day was sunny and there were a lot of people. The music started and it sounded really good. The singer had a beautiful voice and they played well-known songs.

My friend and I danced and sang along with the crowd. The music made us feel very happy and excited. There were people of all ages and everyone joined in to enjoy the concert together.

In addition, there were vendors selling delicious food like hot dogs, nachos, and cotton candy. We bought a little bit of everything and enjoyed the food while the music kept playing.

After a while, an older lady approached us and sat next to us. We started chatting with her and she told us that she also liked the music they were playing. She was a very kind and friendly person.

The concert lasted a couple of hours and ended with a very cheerful song that made everyone stand up and dance. It was a very special moment that I will remember for a long time.

The concert in the park was a day full of music, food, and good company. I would love to go to another concert in the park and live such a fun and exciting experience again.

The Soccer Game

The other day, I went to watch a soccer game with my family. It was a sunny day and very hot, but that didn't stop us from enjoying the game.

There were many fans in the stands, all cheering for their favorite team. The players were very focused on the game and seemed to be enjoying it as much as we were.

The game started and both teams were evenly matched. The players moved quickly across the field, passing the ball back and forth. Goals were made and missed, keeping the excitement high at all times.

My favorite team made a goal and that made us jump for joy in the stands. The excitement of the moment was incredible. All the other fans stood up and started applauding. It was a very special moment.

The game continued and both teams kept playing hard. The game was coming to an end, but no one knew who would win. Finally, one of the teams made another goal, allowing them to win the game.

The excitement in the stadium was indescribable. We were all so happy and excited. The players gathered in the center of the field to congratulate each other and the crowd applauded them.

It was a day full of emotions and positive feelings. The soccer game was a unique experience that I will remember forever.

The family gathering

Yesterday, I had the opportunity to have a family gathering at my grandmother's house. It had been a long time since we had all seen each other together, so we were very excited.

Upon arrival, my grandmother greeted us with a big smile and invited us in. There were many members of my family in the house, all talking and laughing. The atmosphere was very pleasant and warm.

While the food was being prepared, my grandmother told us stories from when she was young. She talked about her childhood and the pranks she used to play with her siblings. We all listened attentively, enjoying her stories.

Finally, the food was ready. We all sat together around the table and started to eat. There were many delicious dishes and the food was exquisite. While we ate, we continued talking and laughing.

After eating, my grandmother brought out an old photo album and started to show it to us. The pictures showed members of our family who were no longer with us, but who will always be in our hearts.

The afternoon flew by and soon we had to say goodbye. We hugged each other, with tears in our eyes, and promised to gather together again soon. It was a wonderful day that we will remember forever.

The Halloween Party

Once upon a time, there was a Halloween party in the neighborhood. Everyone was dressed up in fun and colorful costumes. There were princesses, pirates, and monsters.

The party was decorated with spider webs, pumpkins, and colorful lights. There were exciting games such as ring toss and trick-or-treat scavenger hunt.

Everyone ate delicious treats like candies and chocolates. There was also cheerful music that everyone danced to.

At the end of the party, there was a costume contest and everyone voted for their favorites. It was a fun night and everyone went home with smiles on their faces and lots of candies in their bags.

The Thanksgiving Day Parade

Once upon a time, there was a small town that was very excited for the arrival of Thanksgiving Day. Everyone was planning the big parade that was going to pass through the streets of the city. There were marching bands, giant floats, and people in costumes.

Ana's grandmother was very excited for the parade. She remembered how she used to watch the parades with her parents when she was young. Ana and her family decided to take the grandmother to see the parade in the front row.

When they arrived at the parade, Ana's grandmother was very excited. She could feel the music vibrating in her heart and the positive energy of the crowd. The grandmother smiled from ear to ear as she watched the floats pass by and the dancers dance to the music.

After the parade, Ana's grandmother was very happy and grateful for having had the opportunity to witness the parade. Ana's family decided to end the day with a Thanksgiving dinner at their home, where they shared a delicious meal and remembered all they had to be thankful for.

Ana's grandmother was very happy to have spent the day with her family, reminiscing old times and creating new memories.

The Christmas at My House

When I was a child, Christmas at my house was the best time of the year. I loved waking up early in the morning and running to the living room to see the presents under the Christmas tree.

My mother always prepared a delicious Christmas breakfast that included gingerbread, cookies, and hot chocolate. My father and I played Christmas music and sang carols while my mother cooked.

After breakfast, my family and I dressed up in our best clothes and went to church for Christmas mass. I loved seeing the church decorated with lights and garlands, and hearing the choirs sing carols.

After mass, we came back home to open the presents. I loved seeing the joy on my family's faces when they opened their gifts. My grandmother always made handmade gifts, and I cherished mine.

For Christmas dinner, my mother cooked a big and delicious turkey, along with mashed potatoes, cranberry sauce, and many other treats. After dinner, my family and I sat around the Christmas tree and shared stories and laughs.

Christmas at my house has always been a special time of love, joy, and happiness. Although I am older now, I still feel that excitement when I think of those times when I was surrounded by my family at Christmas.

The arrival of winter

The arrival of winter is my favorite time of year. I love seeing the snowflakes falling slowly from the sky and the white snow covering the whole landscape. I enjoy the sound of the crisp leaves under my feet as I walk down the street.

Every time winter arrives, my family and I prepare for the holidays. We gather around the fireplace, eat delicious meals, and drink hot beverages while sharing stories and memories from the past.

One of my favorite winter traditions is making snowmen with my children and grandchildren. I teach them how to put together three snowballs to make the head, body, and legs, and then we decorate our snowmen with hats, scarves, and carrots for the nose.

I also like to take walks in the park and watch children slide down hills on sleds and skate on ice. The laughter and smiles of the children make me feel very happy and fill me with joy.

As the days get shorter and the nights get colder, I know that winter has officially arrived. But for me, the arrival of winter is a special time filled with happy memories and joy. I love everything that winter brings and I am excited to experience it once again this year.

Valentine's Day

Hi! My name is Jennifer, and today I want to tell you my story of Valentine's Day. This is my favorite day of the year because I celebrate love and friendship with all the people I love.

At my home, we always prepare something special for this day. My husband gives me flowers and chocolates, and I cook his favorite dinner. After dinner, we take a walk in the park and enjoy the cool breeze and the stars in the sky.

But I don't just celebrate love with my husband, I also celebrate it with my friends and family. Sometimes, we organize a party and share stories and memories. I love seeing the smiles on their faces and feeling the love in the air.

I remember when I was a child, my grandmother told me stories about true love and how to find your soulmate. I loved listening to her and dreaming of finding my prince charming. And now that I've found him, I couldn't be happier.

Valentine's Day is an opportunity to remember that love and friendship are the most important things in life. I love celebrating it every year and I'm looking forward to the next one.

Mother's Day

Mother's Day is one of my favorites. I love it because it's a day to thank the person who gave me life. My mom is the best in the world, she's always been there for me. She's taught me so many things, from how to cook to how to be a good person.

I remember that on Mother's Day, my dad and I would make her breakfast in bed. My dad would cook eggs and bacon while I made orange juice and toasted bread. After we ate together, my mom would open her gifts. I always gave her a card that I made at school and a plant for her garden.

In the afternoon, the whole family would gather at my grandmother's house to celebrate. There was lots of delicious food, music, and laughter. My mom was always surrounded by her siblings and nieces and nephews, everyone telling her how much they loved her.

Now that my mom is no longer with us, I like to remember those happy days. I like to think about how she enjoyed her special day surrounded by love and affection. I miss her very much, but I feel like her spirit is with me on every Mother's Day.

Father's Day

Today is a very special day, it's Father's Day. I really like this day because I can give my dad a gift and tell him how much I love him.

I like to think about all the things my dad does for me. He always helps me with my homework, takes me to the park to play soccer, tells me bedtime stories, and gives me big hugs. Sometimes he also takes me out for ice cream or to watch a funny movie.

Today I want to do something special for him. I have prepared his favorite breakfast: scrambled eggs with bacon and orange juice. In addition, I have made a card with lots of colors and written a very nice message on it.

When I give him the gift, my dad looks at me with a big smile on his face. He hugs me and tells me that I am his most precious gift. That makes me feel very happy and very loved.

Today is a very beautiful day because I can tell my dad how much I love him and how important he is to me. I feel very grateful to have such a loving and caring dad.

The First Date

I was very excited because today was my first date with a girl I liked a lot. I had prepared a lot for this moment, I had chosen my best shirt and pants, I had cut my hair, and I had even put on a little cologne.

We met at a coffee shop, and when I saw her, I knew I had done the right thing by inviting her. She looked beautiful in her flowery dress, and her smile made me feel like I was floating in the air.

We ordered coffee and cake and started talking. We talked about our families, our goals, and our favorite things. We discovered that we had a lot in common and that we liked spending time outdoors. I told her about my love for music, and she showed me some pictures of her dog.

Time flew by, and suddenly, I realized that the coffee shop was about to close. I asked her if she wanted to go for a walk, and she agreed. We walked through the park and admired the full moon. She told me she was having a great time, and I felt a huge relief and happiness hearing that.

Finally, it was time to say goodbye. I told her I had a great time and would love to see her again. She smiled and said she would like that too.

I walked home with a big smile on my face. This had been a wonderful night that I would never forget.

The first kiss

I clearly remember my first kiss. It was on a summer night at my friend's house. There were many people there, but I only had eyes for her. She seemed like the most beautiful girl I had ever seen in my life.

I remember that we danced together, and after a while, she took my hand and led me outside. We walked together through the garden and sat down on a bench under a tree.

We looked into each other's eyes, and suddenly I felt her face getting closer to mine. I closed my eyes and felt her soft lips on mine. It was a magical moment.

That kiss made me feel alive and full of emotion. It was as if the whole universe had aligned to bring me that perfect moment. That memory will always be in my heart.

Although many years have passed since that moment, I can still remember the feeling of her lips on mine. That first kiss was an unforgettable moment in my life.

The Moving Day

I remember the day we moved into our new house. It was both exciting and scary. We had lived in our previous house for many years, and we felt like it was time to start a new adventure.

The moving day was a very busy day. There were boxes everywhere, and it was hard to find the things we needed. But despite all the chaos, it was also a very exciting day. With every box we brought into the new house, we imagined what our life would be like there.

I remember my family and I working together to carry all the boxes into the new house. It was exhausting, but it was also fun to work together. We laughed a lot and felt closer than ever.

Finally, after many hours of hard work, all the boxes were in place. I felt a great sense of relief and also a great excitement. We looked around and realized that we were in our new home.

That day will always be in my memory as a day of changes and new opportunities. Although it was a bit stressful, it was also exciting and full of laughter. Now, years later, we continue to enjoy our home and the memories we have created here.

The wedding day

My wedding day was one of the happiest days of my life. I woke up early in the morning with a feeling of excitement in my stomach. I put on my white dress and did my hair. My friends arrived and we laughed together as we put on our makeup.

When we arrived at the church, my future husband was waiting for me at the altar with a smile. He took my hand and looked into my eyes. We said "I do" in front of our friends and family. Then, we had a big party with music, food, and dancing. We danced together and had a lot of fun.

At the end of the day, we were exhausted but very happy. We went home together, happy to have started a new life together. I will always remember that day with a smile on my face.

The day of a child's birth

Hi, today I want to share a very special story. It's about the day my child was born. It was a day filled with emotions and happiness.

I remember we were at the hospital waiting for the moment when my baby would come into the world. The room was full of light and love. I was a little nervous, but my husband was by my side and gave me strength.

After a while, the long-awaited moment finally arrived. I heard my baby cry and my heart filled with joy. When I saw him for the first time, I knew I would love him forever. He was small and delicate, but had an incredible strength.

I remember holding him in my arms and hugging him with all my love. He was perfect and surrounded by so much love. Since that day, my life changed forever. Every day has been a gift and I am grateful for every moment I have spent with my child.

Now that he is an adult, I remember that day with much emotion and gratitude. I will always be thankful for the blessing of having my child in my life.

Moving to a Retirement Home

Some time ago, my family and I moved to a retirement home. At first, I didn't like the idea of leaving my house, but then I understood that it was the best for me.

In the retirement home, I met many kind and friendly people. We had fun activities every day, such as board games, music, and dancing. We also had exercise classes to keep us healthy and strong.

The best part of it all was that I didn't have to worry about cooking or cleaning. The caregivers took care of all of that and made sure that I always had delicious food and a clean and comfortable room.

In the retirement home, I found a welcoming home full of love. All of the people who worked there cared very much about us and treated us like we were their family. I am very grateful for this experience and happy that I made the decision to move here.

The doctor's visit

My name is Ross and today I want to tell you about my last doctor's visit. I went to the doctor because I had a lot of stomach pain and felt nauseous. I don't like going to the doctor, but my daughter insisted that I go to see what was wrong with me.

When I arrived at the office, I met a very friendly doctor who welcomed me with a smile. He asked me some questions about how I was feeling and then examined me carefully. He did some tests and told me everything was fine.

I felt very relieved to hear this, but the doctor gave me some recommendations to take better care of my health. He told me I needed to eat more fruits and vegetables, drink plenty of water, and exercise every day. He also gave me some pills to help with my stomach pain.

After my visit, I felt better and more at ease. I really liked the way the doctor treated me and I felt well taken care of. I learned that it is important to take care of my health and follow the doctor's recommendations. Sometimes it's hard, but I know it's the best thing for me.

The trip to the beach

I love to remember the trip I took to the beach a few years ago. My family and I rented a little house by the sea, and it was a wonderful experience.

I remember on the way there, we rented a small and cozy house with a beautiful view. When we arrived, we went to the beach and spent hours enjoying the sun and the cool water of the sea.

We also went fishing and ate fresh seafood at nearby restaurants. It was an unforgettable experience.

The sand, the sun, and the sea were so relaxing that for a few days, I didn't think about anything else but enjoying the moment with my family.

I would love to go back to the beach someday and feel the sea breeze and the sound of the waves again.

The Trip to the Mountain

Hi, today I want to tell you about a very exciting trip I had to the mountains. It was a very special adventure for me and I always like to remember it.

A few years ago, my family and I decided to take a trip to the mountains. I remember it was very early in the morning when we left home and got into the car. We drove for several hours and finally arrived at our destination.

Upon arrival, I was amazed at how beautiful the mountain scenery was - it was all green and there were many tall trees. We could breathe fresh air and feel nature all around us.

During the day, we walked along the mountain trails, took pictures, and enjoyed the beautiful views. We also had a picnic in a place with an amazing view. We ate sandwiches, fruit, and drank soft drinks while enjoying the scenery.

After a day full of adventures, we went to our hotel in the mountains. It was a cozy place with a fireplace and an impressive view. We spent the night there, enjoying the quiet atmosphere of the mountains.

It was a very special trip for me and I always like to remember it. Whenever I think about that trip, I feel happy and grateful for having had the opportunity to explore the beauty of nature in the mountains with my family.

The trip to the countryside

Hi! My name is John and I want to tell you my story about the trip I took to the countryside.

A few years ago, my family and I decided to take a trip to the countryside to enjoy nature. We woke up early in the morning and packed all our things to spend a few days in the countryside.

When we arrived, the air was fresh and smelled like freshly cut grass. I could see many trees, flowers, and animals. I felt very excited and happy to be there.

During our trip, we went for a walk in the countryside and I saw cows, horses, sheep, and many other animals. We also went fishing in a nearby river and prepared a delicious dinner with the fish we had caught.

At night, my family and I sat around a campfire and told stories. I could see the sky full of stars and listen to the sound of crickets. It was a very peaceful and relaxing night.

The next day, we went for another walk in the countryside and discovered new things. We took photographs and enjoyed the beauty of nature.

It was a wonderful trip that I will always remember. I loved being surrounded by nature and spending time with my family. It was a very pleasant experience and I hope to have the opportunity to take a similar trip again in the future.

The Adventure in the Forest

One sunny day, my family and I decided to go on an adventure in the forest. I was very excited because I love nature and animals.

When we arrived in the forest, we walked along a trail surrounded by tall, green trees, listening to the sound of birds singing. Suddenly, we saw a cute little animal running down the path. It was a bunny and we stopped to watch it.

We continued walking and found a crystal-clear stream where we could cool off and play. Afterwards, we ventured a bit further into the forest and found a small clearing where we rested and enjoyed a picnic.

While we ate, we saw a beautiful deer and many different birds flying around us. My little sister was very excited and couldn't stop laughing and playing with the birds.

After the picnic, we continued walking through the forest and discovered a huge, ancient tree that looked like it was a thousand years old. We were all amazed by its size and beauty. I sat down under the tree and closed my eyes, enjoying the fresh breeze and the sound of the leaves.

Finally, after many hours of walking and exploring, we returned home with many happy memories of our adventure in the forest.

It was a wonderful day where we could enjoy nature and our family. I hope we can return to the forest soon and keep exploring together.

The Treasure Hunt

Hi, my name is Gerald and today I am on a treasure hunt. I remember my grandfather telling me about a treasure hidden in a nearby forest, and he asked me to search for it someday. Today is the day.

I am excited and a little nervous at the same time. What will I find in the forest? Will it be a treasure of gold and shiny jewels, or maybe something more valuable, like friendship and happiness?

I walked along a trail surrounded by tall green trees. The sun was shining and I felt the cool breeze on my face. I listened to the birds singing and the sounds of the forest animals. I felt cheerful and full of energy.

Suddenly, I saw something shiny on the ground. It was a gold coin. I couldn't believe it, maybe I had found the treasure! I kept walking, finding more coins and some precious stones.

As I walked, I realized that the true wealth was not in the gold coins and precious stones, but in the simple things of life. The beauty of nature, the happiness of spending time with friends and family, and the joy of doing something you love.

Finally, I arrived at a clearing in the forest and found a wooden box. I opened it and found a note written by my grandfather. It said, "Dear Gerald, true wealth is not found in gold and jewels, but in the experiences you live and the people you love. I hope your search has taught you this."

I understood what my grandfather meant. The treasure I was looking for was already inside me all the time. I felt grateful and happy.

I returned home with a smile on my face and my heart full of love. I hope this story brought you a sense of happiness and fulfillment. It is never too late to discover the true treasure of life.

Mushroom Hunting

Hello, my name is Ross and today I am excited because I am going mushroom hunting. I love walking through the forest, breathing in the fresh air, and enjoying nature.

I grabbed my basket and started walking along the forest path. As I walked, I heard the sound of the crunchy leaves under my feet and the singing of the birds. I felt happy and peaceful.

After a while, I saw something brown on the ground. It was a large and beautiful mushroom. I picked it up and put it in my basket. I continued walking and found more and more mushrooms of different shapes and sizes. Every time I found one, I felt excited and happy.

As I searched for mushrooms, I also realized how beautiful the forest was. There were tall, green trees, and the sun shone through the leaves. I felt grateful to be surrounded by so much natural beauty.

Finally, I filled my basket with many mushrooms and decided to head back home. I felt satisfied and happy to have found so many delicious mushrooms. I planned to cook a delicious dinner with them and enjoy the food with my family.

I loved my day in the forest and mushroom hunting. I hope to return soon and enjoy the natural beauty that surrounds us. It made me feel happy and grateful for everything I have in my life.

I hope this story brought you a sense of happiness and satisfaction. Enjoying nature is one of the simplest and most beautiful things we can do.

Fishing in the River

Hello, my name is Juan and today I'm excited because I'm going fishing in the river. I love fishing and I hope to catch many fish.

I grabbed my fishing rod and headed to the river. As I walked, I listened to the sound of the water rushing and the singing of the birds. I felt happy and excited for what the day had in store for me.

I arrived at the river and cast my hook. I patiently waited while watching the water, feeling the fresh breeze on my face. Suddenly, I felt a tug on my rod. I had caught a fish!

I pulled the rod and brought a beautiful fish out of the water. I felt excited and happy to see my catch. I decided to release the fish back into the water so it could keep swimming.

I continued fishing and caught more fish. Every time I caught one, I felt excited and grateful for the experience. I enjoyed the sound of the water and the beauty of the surrounding landscape.

Finally, I decided to return home with my day's catch. I felt happy and satisfied for having enjoyed a day of fishing in the river. I planned to cook some of the fish for dinner and share them with my family and friends.

Fishing in the river is an activity that makes me feel happy and excited. I enjoy the tranquility of the water and the natural beauty that surrounds me. I hope to return to the river soon and catch more fish in the future.

I hope this story has brought you a sense of happiness and satisfaction. Enjoying nature and our favorite activities is one of the simplest and most beautiful things we can do in life.

The Afternoon at the Park

Hi, my name is Abella and today I decided to go to the park. I like coming here because I can enjoy the sun, fresh air, and nature. Plus, I can see many people and children playing and having fun.

I arrived at the park and walked along the trails. I heard the sound of birds and leaves rustling in the wind. I felt happy and relaxed by the peacefulness of the place.

I found a bench and sat down to rest. I looked around and saw children playing in the playground. I liked seeing them laughing and having fun together. I also saw some older people walking and talking with each other.

Suddenly, a child approached me and asked if I wanted to play with him. I felt happy and grateful for his kindness. I played with him for a while and had a lot of fun. The child said goodbye to me and went to play with his friends.

I continued walking through the park and found a garden full of flowers. I approached them and observed them for a while. I loved seeing the different colors and shapes of the flowers.

Finally, I decided to go back home after enjoying a wonderful afternoon at the park. I felt happy and grateful for the time I spent in touch with nature and the people I met there.

The afternoon at the park is an experience that makes me feel happy and relaxed. I enjoy the beauty of the place and the people and children around me. I hope to come back soon to the park and continue enjoying nature and the people who inhabit it.

I hope this story brought you a sense of happiness and satisfaction. Enjoying nature and our relationships with others is one of the simplest and most beautiful things we can do in life.

The Snow Day

Hi, my name is Jack and today was a very special day. Do you want to know why? Because it snowed. Yes, it snowed! It's one of the most beautiful things I've ever seen.

When I woke up this morning, I saw that everything was covered in snow. The houses, the trees, the cars, everything was covered in a soft white blanket. I felt so excited to see the snow, so I dressed warmly and went out for a walk.

I walked down the street and saw many people who were also enjoying the snow. I saw some children playing with sleds and making snowballs. I also saw some adults walking their dogs and taking pictures.

I stopped at a park and saw some people who were building a snowman. I approached them and helped them finish it. It was so much fun playing with the snow and creating something so beautiful.

After playing with the snow, I walked to a café and had a hot chocolate to warm up. I felt very comfortable and cozy with the warm cup in my hands. I could feel how the hot chocolate warmed up my body.

Finally, I returned home after enjoying a beautiful snow day. I felt very happy to have been able to enjoy something so beautiful and unexpected. I hope it snows again soon so that I can enjoy this beautiful spectacle of nature once again.

The snow day was a very special day for me. I enjoyed the beauty of the snow and the people who were around me. I hope to see the snow again soon and be able to enjoy its beauty once again.

The Day of the Rain

Hi, my name is Samantha. Today has been a very special day because it has been raining. I love the rain because it makes everything look fresh and clean. I want to tell you what I did during the day of the rain.

When I woke up this morning, I saw that it was raining a lot. I looked out the window and saw how the rain was falling on the trees and buildings. I loved the way the raindrops made everything look brighter and more alive.

I took my umbrella and went for a walk in the rain. I love walking in the rain because I can feel the fresh water drops on my face and hear the gentle sound of the rain falling on my umbrella.

I walked to a small café that I really like. I ordered a cup of hot tea and sat by the window to watch the rain. I loved the way the raindrops made everything look cozier and warmer. The hot cup of tea helped me warm up and feel more comfortable.

After finishing my tea, I walked to a nearby park. I loved the way the tree leaves looked fresh and shiny because of the rain. I could see some flowers that had come out after the rain, and I loved the way the water had made them look brighter.

Finally, I returned home after enjoying a beautiful day of rain. I felt very happy to have been able to enjoy something so beautiful and unexpected. I hope it rains again soon so that I can enjoy the beauty of the rain once again.

The day of the rain was a very special day for me. I enjoyed the beauty of the rain and the things around me. I hope to see the rain again soon and be able to enjoy its beauty once again.

The Windy Day

Hello, my name is Paul. Today has been a very special day because it has been very windy. I want to tell you what I did during the day of the wind.

When I woke up this morning, I saw that it was very windy. I looked out the window and saw how the leaves on the trees were moving back and forth. I loved how the wind made everything seem more exciting and fun.

I took my kite and went to a nearby park. I love flying kites when it's windy because I can feel the strength of the wind in my kite and in my body. I loved seeing how my kite moved back and forth in the sky and how the wind blew around me.

After flying my kite, I walked to a place where I could see how the leaves on the trees were moving back and forth in the wind. I loved the way the leaves rustled and collided with each other in the wind. It made me feel like I was in a magical and exciting place.

Finally, I returned home after enjoying a beautiful day of wind. I felt very happy to have been able to enjoy something so beautiful and unexpected. I hope the wind will blow again soon so I can enjoy its beauty again.

The day of the wind was a very special day for me. I enjoyed the excitement and strength of the wind and the things that were around me. I hope to feel the wind again soon and be able to enjoy its beauty again.

A starry night

Hello, my name is Rachelle. I want to tell you about a very special night for me. It was a starry night and it made me feel very happy.

I went out for a walk at night and saw that the sky was full of stars. I loved seeing how the stars shone in the sky and how the sky seemed magical and exciting.

As I walked, I thought about all the beautiful things in the world. I thought about my family and friends, my pets, and all the things that make me happy. It made me feel very grateful for having all these things in my life.

I continued walking and saw how the moon shone in the sky. I loved seeing how the moon illuminated everything around me and how everything seemed more beautiful under its light.

Finally, I returned home after enjoying a very beautiful starry night. I felt very happy and grateful for everything I have in my life and for being able to enjoy the beauty of the starry night.

The starry night was a very special night for me. It made me feel happy and grateful for all the beautiful things I have in my life. I hope that someday you can enjoy a starry night like I did.

The night out dancing

Hi, my name is Thomas. I want to tell you about a very special night for me. I went out dancing with my friends and it was a really fun night.

I got dressed up and wore my best clothes for the night. When I arrived at the dance venue, I heard the music and saw how everyone was happy and dancing together. I enjoyed seeing everyone enjoying the music and having a good time.

I joined my friends and we started dancing together. We danced to the beat of the music and had a lot of fun together. I loved feeling the music in my body and seeing everyone dancing together in harmony.

After dancing, my friends and I sat down and ordered some drinks. We talked and laughed together, reminiscing about the fun things we had done together. It was a very special night for me because I was able to spend a pleasant time with my friends and forget about everyday problems.

Finally, it was time to go home. I felt very grateful for the night I had just experienced and for having had the opportunity to dance and have a good time with my friends.

The night out dancing was a very special night for me. I danced, laughed, and enjoyed the company of my friends. I hope to have another night like this soon.

The Cinema Visit

Today, my son took me to the cinema. He knew how much I loved watching movies when I was younger and wanted to reminisce those times with me. Although I was a bit nervous about going out, my son assured me that everything would be alright.

When we arrived at the cinema, I was impressed by how big and beautiful it was. My son bought the tickets and then took me to my seat. We sat together and he explained to me how the cinema worked.

The movie was funny and exciting. I laughed and enjoyed every moment. I felt so happy to be there with my son, sharing this moment together.

After the movie, my son bought me popcorn and a drink. We talked about the movie while enjoying our treats. It was a special day that I will never forget. I am grateful to my son for taking me to the cinema and making me feel young again.

The dinner at the restaurant

Hello, today I want to tell you about the time I went to have dinner at a restaurant with my family. We were all very excited to go to this special place where the food is delicious and the atmosphere is pleasant. Upon arrival, we were greeted by a friendly waiter who showed us to our table and gave us the menu so we could choose what we liked.

I ordered my favorite dish, a tasty roasted chicken with vegetables and a fresh salad. And to drink, a refreshing lemonade. The dinner was delicious, but the best part was sharing that moment with my family. We talked, laughed, and remembered old anecdotes. We even took a photo to keep the memory.

At the end, the waiter brought us the bill and we paid. It was a very special day that I will remember with great affection. I hope you enjoyed this story as much as I enjoyed that dinner at the restaurant.

The afternoon at the café

Hi, my name is Sophia. Today, I want to tell you about a very special afternoon I spent in a café with my friends. We went to a cozy place where you could smell the freshly brewed coffee in the air. The music was soft and relaxing, which made me feel very calm.

We sat at a table near the window and ordered some delicious apple pies and coffee. As we talked, I could hear the sound of people chatting and laughing around me. I felt like I was in a very cozy place.

I remembered when I was young and used to go to coffee shops with my friends after school. Sometimes, we would stay until late, laughing and talking about our lives. It was a very fun time.

The afternoon at the café with my friends made me feel like I was young again and surrounded by my friends once more. It was a very special afternoon that I will always remember fondly.

The shopping day

Today is a special day, my daughter is taking me shopping at the mall.

I feel excited because it's been a long time since I've been out of the house. We walked together through the stores and had a lot of fun looking for new clothes and shoes.

I tried on many things and liked some, but not others. Finally, I found a blouse that fits me perfectly and a comfortable pair of shoes that I loved.

My daughter bought me an ice cream as a reward for behaving well in the store. It was a beautiful day and I am happy to have spent it with my daughter.

The Visit to the Amusement Park

Hi! Today I want to share with you a very fun story that happened to me some time ago at an amusement park.

It was a beautiful and sunny day, so I decided to go to the amusement park with my family. There were many exciting rides, roller coasters, bumper cars, carousels, and many other games. Everything was so exciting that I didn't know what to do first.

My grandson, who always entertains me, invited me to ride the roller coaster. At first, I was a little scared, but then I felt very excited - it was an incredible adventure! I screamed so much that I lost my voice, but I felt very happy and full of energy.

After the roller coaster, we tried the bumper cars - it was so much fun! My husband and I bumped into each other many times and laughed non-stop. Then we went on the carousel, and I felt like a little girl again, spinning and spinning while the music played.

Later, we walked around the park and enjoyed the view of the gardens and people having fun on the rides. We ate some sweets and had a soda to refresh ourselves.

It was a wonderful day full of emotions. I felt so happy and grateful to have a family who loves and cares for me. It was a day that I will never forget and always remember with fondness.

How fun it is to visit an amusement park! I hope to go back soon and have more exciting adventures with my family.

The Visit to the Zoo

One sunny morning, my family and I went to the zoo. I was very excited to see the animals, especially the lions.

When we arrived, we walked down a path and saw many different animals. I saw giraffes, monkeys, and a huge elephant. It was amazing!

Finally, we arrived at the lion section. I heard one roar and I got a little scared, but mom assured me that everything was okay. I saw a lazy lion lying on a rock, and another one pacing back and forth in its cage. I was impressed by how strong and majestic they were.

After that, we got some ice cream and continued exploring the zoo. It was a wonderful day, full of emotions and adventures.

I hope you enjoyed the story. Visiting the zoo is an exciting and fun experience, and there is always something new to discover.

The visit to the aquarium

I'm excited to go to the aquarium today. I really like seeing fish and all marine animals. My friends drove me there and helped me get out of the car. The aquarium was crowded, but I was able to see many fish and marine animals that I loved. I saw dolphins, penguins, and many other creatures. Some were very small and others were huge. I was very impressed to see the way they move in the water.

We walked slowly through the underwater tunnels and I marveled at the different types of fish swimming around me. The colors were beautiful and I loved seeing them move. I also really enjoyed the shark area, although my friend assured me we were completely safe.

After seeing everything, we sat in a small café to have a drink and rest for a while. I felt very happy and grateful to have come to this wonderful place. It was an incredible experience and I will always remember this day.

The day at the museum

Today I went to the museum with my family. There were many interesting things there.

I loved the paintings and sculptures. I also learned many new things. My grandson explained to me what each thing was and how it was made.

I felt very fortunate to have such a good family that takes me to such fun places. When we finished our museum visit, we went to eat ice cream.

It was a very hot day and the ice cream refreshed me. It was a very enjoyable day at the museum.

Visit to the Planetarium

Today, I went to a very special place called the "Planetarium."

There, I was able to see a sky full of stars and planets that shone like diamonds. I felt like I was floating in space.

There was a very kind lady who explained everything to us about the stars and planets. I found it fascinating to know that there are thousands of galaxies in the universe and each one is different and unique.

In addition, I watched a movie on a giant screen that made me feel like I was flying among the stars.

It was a wonderful experience, full of colors and emotions. I feel very lucky to have been able to go, and I will remember it for a long time.

Painting Day

Today was a special day because I spent it painting. I really enjoy painting, and today was a lot of fun. I went to the park with my family and we brought all of our paints and brushes.

We sat on a bench next to a lake and started to paint. I painted a landscape with trees and mountains, and also drew some animals. My granddaughter painted a beautiful sun, and my son-in-law painted a bridge.

We were all very focused on our paintings, but we also enjoyed the sun and fresh air in the park. It was very peaceful and relaxing. Every once in a while, someone would make a joke or tell a funny story, and we would all laugh.

After a while, we realized it was time to go home for dinner. We were all happy with our paintings and eager to show them to others. It was a very special and enjoyable day, and I am looking forward to doing it again soon.

A Visit to the Mall

It was a sunny day and my friend Rose had invited me to go to the mall. I felt excited because I love walking around and seeing stores, although I wasn't sure what we might find there.

Upon arriving at the mall, the first thing I noticed was the decor. There were bright lights and eye-catching colors everywhere. It made me feel like I was at a party.

Rose and I started walking and exploring the different stores. I saw many things that I liked, such as clothes, shoes, and jewelry. Rose helped me choose some new things and also bought me a delicious ice cream.

After shopping, we sat on a bench and rested for a bit. I felt very happy to be there with my friend. We talked and laughed together, and that made me feel very good.

Finally, it was time to go home. I said goodbye to Rose and thanked her for a wonderful day. I even received some gifts that she bought for me. I felt grateful and happy, and thought it had been a great adventure.

Candlelit Dinner

A few days ago, my grandson invited me over for dinner at his house. When I arrived, he surprised me with a beautiful table set with candles and a delicious meal.

He had prepared everything with so much love and care that it moved me deeply. We ate together and talked about many things, reminiscing on anecdotes and happy moments we had shared together.

The dinner was very special and I will never forget it. Sometimes, the simplest and most ordinary moments can be the most memorable.

Board Game Afternoon

Today is a special day because my friends and I are going to have a fun afternoon playing board games. I am very excited to see them and spend time with them.

When my friends arrive, we greet each other with hugs and smiles. We decide to play the card game that we all enjoy. While we play, we talk and laugh together. I feel very happy to be with them.

After playing the card game, we decide to play chess. Some of my friends really like this game, and I love it too. Although I'm not very good, I have a lot of fun trying to win.

While we play chess, we take a break to eat some cookies and drink soda. I enjoy watching my friends enjoy the food and laughing together.

Finally, we end the afternoon with another board game that is very fun. We laugh so much that our stomachs hurt. When we say goodbye, we hug and kiss each other on the cheek.

Today has been a very special day. I have loved spending time with my friends, playing board games and laughing together. I am very grateful to have wonderful friends and spend time with them.

The Workout Session

Today I had a workout session and I had a lot of fun. I got up early and put on comfortable clothes. Then I went to the gym with my personal trainer. We did several exercises together and it was a lot of fun.

First, we did warm-up exercises to prepare our bodies. Then we did some strength exercises, lifting weights and moving our arms and legs. I loved feeling my body working and getting in shape.

Afterwards, we did some balance and coordination exercises. We did some yoga poses and I liked feeling calm and relaxed.

Finally, we did some stretches to cool down our bodies. I felt relaxed and at peace.

It was a great workout session! I enjoyed being in shape and feeling good. I'm excited to do it again soon.

The Dance Class

Once upon a time, there was a dance class where people of all ages participated. They were taught how to dance to different types of music and everyone had a great time.

The dance teacher was a very cheerful and friendly woman who always had a smile on her face. She taught her students the steps and movements for each song, and everyone tried their best to imitate her.

The students worked hard to learn, but the most important thing was to enjoy the dance. To the rhythm of the music, they let themselves be carried away and had a lot of fun.

One of the songs they enjoyed dancing to the most was a lively salsa song. Everyone started dancing at the same time and a very festive atmosphere was created.

After the dance class, all the students stayed for a drink and a chat. They laughed as they remembered the steps and talked about how much fun they had.

So, every week they eagerly awaited the next dance class to enjoy the music and the company of their friends.

The Yoga Class

Once upon a time, there was a yoga class in a beautiful and peaceful park. The trees provided shade and the sound of birds created a relaxing atmosphere. The yoga teacher was named Alexa and she was very kind. She had organized the class so that everyone could participate regardless of their skill level.

There were several people in the class, all with different ages and abilities. Alexa started teaching the basic yoga postures, such as the tree pose and the downward-facing dog pose. Everyone followed her instructions and focused on their breathing. They felt relaxed and happy.

Then, the class continued with more advanced postures. Alexa helped those who needed assistance to achieve the correct postures. Everyone made an effort and felt very proud of themselves at the end of the class. They realized that they had improved their flexibility and strength.

The class ended with a meditation guided by Alexa. Everyone closed their eyes and breathed deeply. They felt at peace and grateful for having had the opportunity to participate in the yoga class. They left the park feeling rejuvenated and with a smile on their faces.

The Relaxation Session

Once upon a time, there was a special relaxation session in a calm and cozy place. The air was filled with the scent of lavender and the light was dim and soft. In the center of the room, there were comfortable pillows to sit on and a blanket to keep warm. A very kind person guided us through a relaxation practice.

We started by closing our eyes and taking deep breaths. They asked us to imagine a beautiful and peaceful place inside of us, something that made us feel happy and safe. Then, they led us through a guided relaxation that allowed us to feel more calm and rested.

When the session ended, we felt renewed and full of positive energy. It was a moment of peace and calm that made us feel very good.

A Day at the Spa

Once upon a time, there was a lady named Julia who was spending a day at the spa. She had planned this for a long time and was very excited about her special day.

First, Julia received a relaxing massage. The therapist covered her with scented oils and gently massaged her to help her relax. Julia closed her eyes and felt all the tensions in her body disappear.

Then, she soaked in a hot tub. The hot water made her feel warm and happy. Julia looked at the bubbles floating around her and felt like she was floating on a cloud.

After that, Julia relaxed in a steam room. The hot steam made her sweat and breathe deeply, which helped to eliminate any stress and worries she might have had. It felt like she was breathing in fresh and clean air.

Finally, Julia received a facial treatment. The esthetician applied scented creams and lotions to her face, which made her feel beautiful and special. Julia looked at herself in the mirror and was surprised at how good she looked.

When Julia returned home, she felt like a new person. She felt relaxed, rejuvenated, and happy. She decided that she would return to the spa soon to experience that feeling again.

A Day at the Beauty Salon

Once upon a time, there was a woman named Kate who had planned a special day to go to the beauty salon. She had been looking forward to this day for a long time. Kate got up early that morning, dressed in her prettiest clothes, and headed to the beauty salon.

When she arrived, the hairstylist greeted her with a smile and asked her what she wanted to do. Kate decided to get a haircut and a manicure. While getting her hair cut, the hairstylist talked with Kate about her life and interests. Kate felt very comfortable and enjoyed the conversation.

Then, Kate went to the manicure station, where they applied a beautiful pink nail polish. While waiting for it to dry, she looked at herself in the mirror and felt very happy with her new haircut and pretty nails.

Finally, when they finished, Kate said goodbye to the hairstylist and left the beauty salon. She felt very happy and proud of her appearance and headed home with a smile on her face.

Since then, Kate always remembered that special day when she took the time to take care of herself and feel beautiful.

Crafting Afternoon

Once upon a sunny afternoon, a group of friends gathered in the garden of one of their homes. They had decided to spend the afternoon doing crafts.

There were colored papers, glue, scissors, glitter, and many more things. Everyone got to work and started creating. One made a drawing of a tree, another an airplane, and a friend made a beautiful bead necklace.

As they worked, there were laughter and lively conversations. At the end of the afternoon, each one proudly showed what they had created. It was amazing how everyone had used the same materials but created completely different things.

They felt happy to have spent a fun afternoon together, and each one took their artwork home to remember that special moment.

The Sewing Afternoon

Once upon a time, there was a grandmother named Martha who used to spend her afternoons sitting in her armchair. But one day, her granddaughter invited her to an afternoon of sewing. Martha was very excited, as she had always loved to sew but hadn't done it in a long time.

Her granddaughter took her to a place full of fabrics and colors, where there was a group of women laughing and chatting while they sewed. Martha sat at a table and began to look at the pattern designs and choose the fabrics she liked the most.

Little by little, she began to sew with the other women and share stories and laughs with them. The grandmother felt very happy to be surrounded by so much joy and creativity. In addition, she realized that she had lost track of time and that hours had passed while sewing.

At the end of the afternoon, Martha went home with a beautiful bag she had sewn and filled with emotions and new friendships. The grandmother had never imagined that a sewing afternoon could be so fun and exciting. From that day on, she started going to sewing afternoons with her granddaughter every week, and she always came back home with new creations and a smile on her face.

Embroidery Afternoon

Once upon a sunny afternoon, the grandmother felt a little lonely. Then, she remembered she had an embroidery that had been waiting to be finished for some time. She searched for the materials and began working on it, recalling all the stitches and techniques she had learned in the past.

As she worked on her embroidery, the grandmother felt calm and focused, enjoying the creative process. Suddenly, her young granddaughter came to visit and was amazed at how beautiful the embroidery was turning out. The granddaughter was very interested in learning how to embroider, so the grandmother taught her some tricks and techniques while continuing her work.

The afternoon flew by as the grandmother and granddaughter worked on their projects together. Finally, when the sun began to set, the grandmother realized that she had finished her embroidery. She felt very happy and proud of her work, and thanked her granddaughter for accompanying her and making the afternoon a memorable experience.

The grandmother decided to frame her embroidery and put it on the wall in her living room, where she would admire it every time she passed by. Every time she saw it, she remembered the embroidery afternoon she spent with her granddaughter and felt happy and grateful for that beautiful memory.

The Weaving Afternoon

Once upon a sunny afternoon, a group of friends gathered at the grandmother's house for a weaving afternoon. They all brought their yarn and needles, and the grandmother taught everyone how to weave. At first, some felt a little clumsy, but the grandmother patiently showed them how to do it, and soon everyone began to make beautiful weavings.

As they weaved, they shared stories and laughter, and enjoyed some delicious cookies that the grandmother had baked. After a while, they realized that they had made a lot of progress in their weavings. The colors and textures of the yarn were beautiful and created interesting patterns.

The afternoon flew by as everyone continued weaving, chatting, and having fun. When the sun began to set, the grandmother suggested they take a photo to remember their time together. They grouped together for the photo and smiled, feeling happy and satisfied with their work.

They all promised to meet again for another weaving afternoon and the grandmother said she would be delighted to teach them new patterns and techniques. With their arms full of beautiful weavings, they said goodbye, happy and grateful for an afternoon full of fun and learning.

The pottery afternoon

Once upon a time, a group of friends gathered at a special place to do pottery. They loved creating things with their own hands. The afternoon was sunny and perfect for spending time together and creating something beautiful.

First, the friends sat around a table with clay and began making different shapes with their hands. Some made plates, others bowls, and some made vases. The friends laughed and had fun as they worked together.

After a while, they began to decorate their creations with paint and other materials. Some used bright colors and others used soft colors, but all were beautiful in their own way.

Finally, when they finished creating their pieces, they left them to dry in the sun. The friends sat in the garden and enjoyed a snack while they waited for their pieces to dry.

When the pieces were dry, the friends took them home and put them in a special place to remember that fun afternoon. Every time the friends looked at their pieces, they remembered the time they spent together and felt happy.

Painting Afternoon

Once upon a time, a group of friends met every week to do different activities. One day, they decided they wanted to try something new and exciting, so they organized a painting afternoon.

Each of them received a blank canvas and a color palette. They also had different brushes and tools to help them create their works of art. During the painting session, music played softly in the background, creating a calm and relaxing atmosphere.

The friends immersed themselves in their paintings, using their skills and creativity to create something unique and beautiful. Some painted landscapes of mountains and rivers, while others drew flowers and animals. There was even one who painted a portrait of their loved one.

As the afternoon progressed, each friend was surprised at how much fun they were having. Painting had given them a way to express their emotions and feelings in a different way. At the end of the session, each had created something beautiful and unique.

The friends were very happy and proud of their work, and planned to have another painting afternoon soon. For them, it was a wonderful way to spend an afternoon and create unforgettable memories.

Drawing Afternoon

Once upon a sunny afternoon, a group of friends gathered to enjoy a drawing session. The room was filled with colored pencils, blank sheets of paper, and soft background music.

Everyone sat comfortably and began to draw what inspired them. One drew a tree, another an animal, and another person drew a flower. There was a great atmosphere of creativity and joy in the room, and everyone enjoyed the moment.

While drawing, they recalled happy moments from their childhood, such as when they used to draw with their parents or friends in school. They talked about their favorite colors and how relaxing it was to draw.

The afternoon flew by, and before they knew it, they had created a lot of beautiful and colorful drawings. They felt happy and satisfied to have spent such a pleasant time together.

In the end, they decided to give their drawings to a nearby nursing home so that other people could enjoy their art. Everyone said goodbye with a smile on their face and promised to meet again soon for another drawing afternoon.

The Photography Afternoon

Once upon a time, a group of friends at a senior center had a visitor who brought along their camera and suggested they have some fun taking photos in the garden.

At first, some of them were a bit shy, but then they realized how enjoyable it was. They all started taking photos of flowers, trees, birds, each other, and anything they liked. They even took some group photos together.

After a while, the volunteer showed them how to view the photos on the camera screen, and everyone was thrilled to see what they had captured.

It was a wonderful afternoon filled with laughter and fun, and the friends were grateful for the opportunity to experiment with photography. They decided to print some of the photos as keepsakes.

Since then, whenever they can, they gather in the garden to take photos and enjoy the fresh air. They know that it doesn't matter if the photos are not perfect; what matters is the moment they shared together.

The Video Game Afternoon

Hi, I'm Melissa and today I want to share my experience of a very fun afternoon I spent with my grandchildren playing video games.

Video games are one of the things my grandchildren enjoy the most, and although I didn't understand them much at first, I decided to learn so that I could share that moment with them.

So, a few days ago, my grandchildren taught me how to play a game where we had to collect fruits and vegetables in a garden. At first, it seemed difficult to me, but my grandchildren helped me understand the instructions and little by little, I got better.

The afternoon flew by, we laughed a lot and I was surprised at how much fun I was having. My grandchildren were happy to see that I was also enjoying the game and their company.

I even dared to play another game where we had to dance to the rhythm of the music. It was a bit challenging for me at first, but my grandchildren helped me keep up with the beat, and believe it or not, I danced the whole song!

It was a very fun afternoon, full of positive emotions. I learned something new and enjoyed the company of my grandchildren. I would definitely repeat this experience of the video game afternoon.

The Music Afternoon

My name is Maggie and I'm 78 years old. I'm a cheerful person and I've always loved music. Today has been a very special afternoon because I spent my time listening to my favorite songs. Early in the morning, I woke up with the idea of wanting to listen to music, so I asked my daughter to help me find my old record player. We found it in the attic, covered in dust, but it still worked.

My daughter helped me select some records from my collection and we placed them on the record player. The music started playing and I felt my body filling with energy. I began humming the songs and my daughter joined me. We sang together the songs from my youth, some that I had already forgotten.

I remembered special moments from my life, dances with my husband and family afternoons. The music made me feel happy and made me forget my worries. I danced and sang until I got tired, and then my daughter prepared a small picnic with cookies and lemonade. We enjoyed the picnic while we kept listening to music.

It was a very special afternoon, an afternoon of memories and emotions. The music transported me to past times and filled me with joy. Now I'm tired but happy, and I know I'm going to sleep well tonight, dreaming of songs and happy moments.

Singing Afternoon

Hi, today I want to tell you about the afternoon I spent singing with my friends. We all gathered in the living room, each with a microphone in hand. We listened to some old songs on the radio, and then we started singing together.

At first, we were a bit shy, but then we started feeling the music and loosened up. We sang some of our favorite songs from when we were young, and other popular hits.

It was so much fun to see everyone singing and moving to the beat of the music. Even those who didn't remember all the words still joined in and sang what they knew.

The music made us feel joyful and lively, and we all laughed a lot. It was a wonderful afternoon full of laughter, music, and friends. And I'm sure we'll do it again soon.

Karaoke Afternoon

Hi, my name is Sophie and today I had a really fun afternoon at a place called "karaoke". I went with my friends and we had a great time singing songs that we knew. There was a big screen where the lyrics of the songs appeared, so we could all sing together.

We started by singing old songs that we all like, and then some new songs that we didn't know but really enjoyed. There were many songs in Spanish and English, so we could sing the ones we liked the most.

Sometimes, we made mistakes in the lyrics or in the tone of the song, but it didn't matter because we were having fun. My friends and I laughed a lot and encouraged each other to keep singing.

At the end, we sang a song together that is very special to us. It was very exciting to sing it together and see how we all knew the lyrics. I felt very happy and grateful to have friends with whom I can have so much fun.

It was a very fun afternoon at the karaoke and I hope to go back soon.

Old Movies Afternoon

I love spending time with my friends at the nursing home. Today, we decided it would be fun to have an old movies afternoon. We sat together in the common room, and one of my friends brought out a box of DVDs with some of their favorite movies.

We got comfortable in the armchairs, with blankets and pillows to make us more comfortable. We started with a black and white movie that my friend remembered seeing in the theater when he was young. It was fun to watch it with him, as he got excited at every scene and remembered interesting details about the movie.

After that, we decided to watch another movie, this time a comedy. We laughed a lot and commented on the funniest parts. Some of my friends even knew the dialogues by heart.

It was a very pleasant afternoon, and we had a lot of fun remembering past times and enjoying these movies together. I'm glad to be able to share these moments with them and see their happy faces. We'll definitely have to do this more often.

The afternoon of listening to the radio

Hi! My name is Lisa and I want to tell you about my afternoon of listening to the radio. Today, like every day, I woke up early and after breakfast and doing some things at home, I felt tired and wanted to rest. Then I remembered I had my old radio, so I took it out of my closet and turned it on.

I started searching for a radio station that I liked and after tuning in to several stations, I found one that played music from my favorite era. I got excited listening to songs I hadn't heard in a long time, and started singing along with them.

As I listened to the radio, my mind began to wander and I felt like I was in a time machine, traveling back to my youth. I remembered happy and sad moments, but most of all, I remembered the joy I felt when listening to music. I felt so happy and grateful to be able to relive those memories.

Finally, my favorite program ended and I turned off the radio. I felt relaxed and satisfied, as if I had had a very productive afternoon. I realized that listening to the radio is a wonderful way to connect with my past and feel good in the present.

So, if you have a radio at home, turn it on and see where the music takes you.

Afternoon of Writing Letters

This afternoon I feel very happy, I'm writing letters to my friends and family. I love writing letters, it's a way of telling them how much I love them and staying in touch.

First, I take some time to think about what I want to say to them. Sometimes I talk about the things I've been doing lately, like the walk I took with my friend in the park or the delicious meal I made for dinner. Other times I tell them about my favorite memories, like when my family and I went to the beach many years ago.

Then, I grab my paper and favorite pen. I like to write by hand because I feel it's more personal and my friends and family can feel my love in every word.

As I write, I listen to soft music and feel very relaxed. Sometimes I pause to think of a special word I want to use, but I always try to keep it simple. I want it to be easy to read and understand.

When I finish, I close the envelope and stick the stamp. Then, I put the letters in the mailbox for the mail carrier to take.

I feel very happy to have written letters today. I know my friends and family will feel very happy reading them. And I also feel very happy for taking the time to write and stay in touch with the people I love.

An Afternoon of Reading Poetry

Today, I've decided to spend a quiet afternoon enjoying poetry. I've chosen some of my favorite poems to read and let their words fill me with joy.

I start reading the first poem and as I progress, I can feel the music of the words wrap around me and transport me to a world full of emotions and sensations. The images that the poem evokes are so clear that I can see them in front of me as if they were happening in real-time.

I keep reading, and soon I realize that I've been reading for hours. I feel filled with energy and enthusiasm, as if I've discovered a hidden treasure. I can't wait to share these poems with my friends and family so that they too can enjoy the beauty of the words and the emotions they convey.

This has been a wonderful afternoon. Poetry has awakened something in me that had been dormant for a while. It's reminded me that there is so much beauty in the world and that there is always something to look forward to with excitement. I'm looking forward to immersing myself in the worlds that poets create and discovering new emotions and sensations as the afternoon progresses.

The Afternoon of Reciting Poems

Today I had a very special afternoon. I met with my friends in a cozy living room to recite poems. We all shared our favorite poems and it was wonderful to hear how each one of them expressed their emotions.

One of my friends recited a poem about the sea and its waves, and it reminded me of when I went to the beach many years ago. Another friend recited a poem about friendship, and it made me think about how much I value my friends and the importance of spending time together.

I became so emotional while reciting my own poem that I almost shed tears. It was such a beautiful afternoon that I felt grateful for having friends who share my interests and for having the opportunity to participate in an activity that I enjoy so much.

After the afternoon of reciting poems, I realized that poetry is a wonderful way to express our emotions. I would like to recite more poems in the future, and perhaps even write one of my own. I feel very happy and fulfilled after this afternoon.

An Afternoon Playing with Pets

My name is Marie, and today is a very special day for me because I'm spending the afternoon with my friend Lucy. Lucy has a cute and friendly little dog named Moon. I love playing with her and watching her run around the park.

When we arrived at the park, Moon jumped out of her leash and started sniffing around. I pulled out her favorite ball and threw it for her. Moon chased after it, found it, and brought it back to me in her mouth. I loved seeing her so happy.

After playing for a while, we sat on a bench and Moon curled up at our feet. I petted her head and started telling Lucy about my day. Lucy talked about her own things, and I felt so happy to have a friend to share these moments with.

The afternoon flew by, and when the sun started to set, we decided to take one last stroll before leaving. Moon chased after the ball again, and I had fun watching her play.

When it was time to say goodbye, I felt a little sad, but also grateful for having such a lovely afternoon. I said goodbye to Lucy and Moon, promising to get together soon for another fun afternoon.

The Afternoon of Looking at Old Photos

Once upon a time, there was an afternoon when my family and I decided to go through our old photos together. Each of us took out our photo albums and began to flip through them. We reminisced about the good times we had spent together at different times in our lives.

I saw photos of my parents when they were young, pictures of my brother and me when we were babies, and photos of our old pets. I loved seeing how we have all grown over the years and how things around us have changed.

As we looked at the photos, we remembered funny stories and anecdotes from each image. My father told a story about his first car and how it broke down on a highway. We all laughed together.

It was a very pleasant afternoon, and we all enjoyed looking at our photos together. It made me feel happy and grateful for my family and for the good times we have shared over the years.

Puzzle Afternoon

Hi, today I want to share with you a very fun afternoon that I spent doing puzzles. I love doing them, especially when I have company. My grandson came to visit me and brought a puzzle that we had bought together at a game store.

We started putting it together on the living room table. It was a beautiful landscape with many pieces of different colors and shapes. It was a little difficult at first, but we helped each other and soon found the right pace.

Every time we put a piece in its place, we felt very excited. It was like we had solved a little mystery! The background music, a beautiful 60s song, put us in a good mood and reminded us of times past.

Little by little, the puzzle began to take shape and we could see the landscape forming. It looked like a photo of a very peaceful and beautiful place, with mountains and trees.

When we finished, we felt very proud of ourselves. We had worked together to solve a little challenge and create something beautiful. It was a very fun afternoon full of laughter. I hope I can do another puzzle with my grandson soon, it was an unforgettable afternoon!

The afternoon of playing with blocks

Today has been a very fun day. Someone brought me some colorful blocks to play and build things with. I love playing with them, it's like having my own world where I can build anything I want.

First, I built a very tall tower, with many green, yellow and red blocks. Then I built a long bridge, so my friends can cross to the other side without getting wet. After that, I built a very beautiful house, with many windows and a red door. I liked my house a lot and decided to live there with my friends.

My friends and I kept building new things all day. We built a yellow car and a blue boat to sail in the sea. We also built a high mountain to climb and a long and fun slide to glide down.

I loved building things with the blocks. It made me feel happy and proud of everything I created. I like seeing what I've built and remembering everything we've done. Now I'm very tired but happy to have spent a fun afternoon playing with my blocks.

Afternoon of Making Collages

Today I had a very fun afternoon making collages. I love cutting and pasting different materials onto a paper to create something new and beautiful. I was given a box full of magazines, colored paper, scissors, and glue, and I started creating.

First, I cut out many images that I liked. There were photos of flowers, animals, landscapes, and people. There were also words and letters that I found interesting. Then, I started pasting them onto a large piece of paper, playing with colors and shapes to create a unique design.

As I worked, I felt very relaxed and happy. It was as if all the worries of the day disappeared, and I was left with the joy of creating something beautiful. The soft background music helped me stay focused and relaxed.

After a while, my collage was complete. I loved the final result - it was a colorful portrait of things I liked. It was a good time, and I am excited to make another collage soon.

Making collages is a very fun and creative activity that helps me relax and enjoy the present moment. I am very happy to have spent an afternoon like this.

Afternoon of playing with play-dough

Today I had a very fun afternoon playing with play-dough. I love kneading it and shaping it into my creations. I made a little dog, a cat, a tree, and a snail. I enjoy feeling the soft and malleable texture of the play-dough in my hands. It's an activity that relaxes me and makes me feel happy.

When I was a child, I used to play with play-dough with my friends too. We had fun creating all sorts of things and then proudly showing them to our parents. I like to remember those moments of happiness and fun.

Now, although sometimes it's hard for me to remember things, I can still enjoy these simple and creative activities. It makes me feel like I can still create new things and have fun like I used to. Play-dough makes me feel like a child again, and that makes me very happy.

The Afternoon of Playing with Puppets

Today I had a very special afternoon. Instead of staying alone at home, I decided to play with my puppets. In the attic trunk, I found some old friends: a dog, a cat, a clown, and a bunny.

I began to make them talk and move, and suddenly the clown made me laugh with his silly jokes. The dog told me a story of when he was a puppy, and the bunny showed me how to do a little magic trick.

Playing with puppets made me feel like a child again, full of imagination and joy. I forgot about all my problems for a moment and simply enjoyed the present moment.

If you also have puppets at home, I invite you to take them out and have fun with them. You can invent stories and make them come to life in your hands. I assure you that you will feel happy and relaxed. Dare to play like when you were a child!

Afternoon of Making Puppets

Hi! Today I want to tell you about a wonderful afternoon I spent with my family making puppets.

We started by cutting paper and cardboard to create the body and limbs of the puppets. Then, we added eyes and drew smiles on their faces. It was fun to choose colors for their clothes and details to make each puppet unique.

After assembling them, we made a small stage with a box and a cloth as a curtain. Each of us chose a puppet and started creating stories and dialogues. We laughed a lot and had so much fun watching our puppets come to life.

It was a very special afternoon, where imagination and creativity came together to make us happy. Although sometimes it's hard to remember details from a long time ago, the memory of that afternoon always fills me with joy.

The Afternoon of Telling Stories

My name is Meghan and today has been a very special afternoon for me. I gathered with a group of friends in the community room of our home to tell stories.

The atmosphere was warm and welcoming, with comfortable armchairs and a small table with refreshments and cookies. I was very happy to share that moment with my friends, all of whom are very close to my heart.

First, my friend Marie told a story about princesses and castles, with lots of suspense and a happy ending. Then, Max told a story of adventures in the jungle, full of action and dangers. We were all very excited, shouting and applauding at the most intense parts.

When it was my turn, I thought that telling a childhood story would be a good idea. I remembered when my grandmother took me for a walk in the countryside and taught me the names of flowers and animals. Every time I visited her, she surprised me with a new story, full of magic and tenderness.

So I started telling the story of a grandmother and her granddaughter, who went for a walk in the countryside and met a very mischievous rabbit. We named him and gave him a very nice personality. The grandmother and granddaughter spent the whole day playing with him and discovering new places in the countryside. In the end, they found a very special surprise: a nest of freshly laid bird eggs.

I finished the story with a smile, happy to have shared a little piece of my childhood with my friends. Everyone applauded and congratulated me on my story.

It was a very fun and emotional afternoon, full of laughter and joy. I love being able to share these moments with my friends and enjoy the magic of storytelling. I hope we can do it again soon.

The afternoon of making papier-mâché crafts

Today is a sunny day, and I am in the mood for some crafting. My granddaughter has brought me a fun idea to make with papier-mâché, and I am excited to get started.

First, I need to prepare the papier-mâché. My granddaughter has brought me a special mixture that is very easy to make. I simply mix some water and newspaper and stir it until it becomes a smooth paste. Then, I let it sit for a few minutes to settle.

Next, I start creating shapes with the papier-mâché paste. I make a ball and flatten it a bit to become an oval shape. Then, carefully, I fold the edges to make it look like a plate. It's perfect to use as a decoration in my home.

The afternoon flies by as I work on my craft. Sometimes, I feel frustrated because my hands don't want to do what I want them to do. But when I finally manage to create something, I feel very happy. It makes me feel like I can do anything.

Finally, my granddaughter arrives and tells me she is ready to see what I have created. I feel excited to share my work with her. When she sees my papier-mâché plate, her face lights up, and she tells me she loves it. I feel very happy to have created something that I can share with my granddaughter.

This afternoon of crafting has been wonderful. It has allowed me to be creative and has brought joy to my day. Now, I can look forward to our next crafting adventure together.

Afternoon of Making Christmas Decorations

Today is a very special day. My daughter has brought me some things to make Christmas decorations. I love Christmas. It makes me feel happy and brings back memories of my childhood.

First, we start preparing things. My daughter has brought many different colors of paper, scissors, and glue. I like the smell of glue. It reminds me of when I was a child and built things with my father.

We start making the decorations. We make stars and angels with the paper. Sometimes I get confused and forget what I'm doing, but my daughter always helps me and explains what we need to do.

As we make the decorations, we talk about our favorite Christmases. I like listening to my daughter's stories. It makes me feel connected to her and reminds me of the joy that Christmas brings to our lives.

After a while, we have many decorations made. We hang them on the Christmas tree that my daughter has brought. I like seeing the decorations hanging. They remind me of good times and make me feel happy.

This afternoon of making Christmas decorations has been wonderful. It has allowed me to connect with my daughter and remember good times. Now, I can look forward to Christmas and the time we will spend together.

Afternoon of making birthday cards

Today is a very special day because I am making birthday cards with my granddaughter. I enjoy making cards, it makes me feel creative and reminds me of when I was young.

First, my granddaughter and I choose the colors and materials. We pick many bright and beautiful colors. I love how they look together. We also look for some stickers and glitter to add a little sparkle to our cards.

We start making the cards. We cut and paste different shapes and colors onto paper. Sometimes I feel confused, but my granddaughter always helps me and explains what we need to do.

As we make the cards, we talk about the people we will send our cards to. I enjoy listening to my granddaughter talk about her friends and family. It makes me feel connected to her and reminds me of the joy that comes with receiving a birthday card.

After a while, we have many cards made. I like to see how they turned out, they are very pretty. They make me feel happy, knowing that the people who receive them will feel special.

This afternoon of making birthday cards has been wonderful. It has allowed me to connect with my granddaughter and remember good times. Now, I can look forward to the time of sending our cards and making the people who receive them smile.

Afternoon of making cards for friends and family

Today, I decided to make some cards for my friends and family. I enjoy making cards as it's a way of letting the people I care about know that I'm thinking of them.

First, I gathered some materials such as paper, glue, scissors, and colored pencils. I chose beautiful and bright colors to make the cards look special. I love the smell of paper, it reminds me of when I was a child and made crafts with my mother.

I started making the cards by cutting the paper into different shapes and sizes. Then, I began drawing and writing on them. Sometimes I got confused, but I didn't worry too much because I knew there's no wrong way to make a card. I did what came to my mind.

While making the cards, I remembered happy moments I shared with each person I would send a card to. It made me feel very happy to recall those moments.

After a while, I had made many cards. I liked how they looked and how each one was different. It made me feel very good to know that these cards would bring joy to the people I would send them to.

This afternoon of making cards has been very special to me. It has allowed me to recall good times and do something to express my love and affection for the people who matter to me. I'm looking forward to sending these cards and making those who receive them smile.

Afternoon of making rag dolls

Today I decided to make some rag dolls. I love making dolls, it's a way to express my creativity and have fun.

First, I gathered some materials like fabric, thread, needle, stuffing, and buttons. I chose soft fabric and bright colors to make the dolls look beautiful. I love the feeling of soft fabric in my hands.

I started making the dolls. I cut the fabric into different shapes and sizes. Then, I began sewing the different parts of the doll together. Sometimes it was a bit challenging, but I enjoyed the process and didn't worry too much about the final result.

While making the dolls, I thought about the people to whom I would give these dolls. I love the idea of doing something to make them smile and feel special.

After a while, I had many dolls made. I loved how they looked, each one was unique. I felt very happy to have made them and to know that they would bring joy to the people who would receive them.

This afternoon of making rag dolls has been very fun and exciting for me. It has allowed me to feel creative and do something that will bring happiness to others. Now I can look forward to the moment of giving the dolls and seeing the smiles on the faces of those who receive them.

Remembering Old Times

Today, while taking a break in my favorite armchair, I started to remember old times. I remembered my childhood, the games I used to play, and how I used to spend time with my friends and family.

I remember when we played hide and seek, hopscotch, and other fun games. Sometimes we had so much fun that we forgot the time, and our mothers had to come looking for us to go back home.

I also remembered family trips, beach days, and picnics in the park. I loved the smell of sea breeze and the feeling of sand between my toes.

I remembered family meals, where we all gathered around the table and shared stories and laughter. Sometimes there were disagreements, but we always reconciled and ended up enjoying a good dinner together.

I even remembered some sad moments, like when I lost someone close to me. It was difficult at the time, but I remembered how my family and friends were there to support me and help me get through it.

Although my memory may not be as good as it used to be, remembering these old times makes me feel happy and grateful for the experiences I've had. It makes me feel connected to my loved ones and gives me a sense of joy and warmth in my heart.

Remembering old times is something I will always enjoy doing, even if I can't remember everything clearly. It's a reminder that life is full of beautiful moments that will always be with me, regardless of what happens in the future.

The Afternoon of Making Dreamcatchers

Today, I decided to do something different. I wanted to create something with my hands and remembered that I had always wanted to make a dreamcatcher. So, I went to the craft store and bought everything I needed to make one.

I started making my dreamcatcher, tying threads and creating a pattern on the wooden hoop. As I worked on my project, I felt relaxed and focused on the present.

I remembered that my grandmother used to make me dreamcatchers when I was a child. She told me stories about how they caught the bad dreams and let the good ones through. Those stories always made me feel safe and protected.

When I finished my dreamcatcher, I hung it near my bed. I felt very proud of my creation and realized that crafting made me feel happy and satisfied.

I sat down to admire my artwork and closed my eyes. I began to daydream about all the wonderful dreams that awaited me. And in that moment, I realized that my dreamcatcher had done exactly what my grandmother had told me it would do: catch the bad dreams and let the good ones through.

Now, every time I look at my dreamcatcher, I feel happy and grateful for having had the opportunity to create something with my own hands. And although I may not remember everything clearly, I will always remember how making my own dreamcatcher made me feel.

The Waves of the Sea

Today, I went for a walk on the beach and was amazed by the waves of the sea. I loved watching them move and how the sun made them sparkle. I stopped for a moment and closed my eyes, listening to the sound of the waves gently breaking against the shore.

As I watched the sea, I remembered how my family and I used to come to the beach every summer. We spent hours swimming in the sea and playing in the sand. My brother and I used to build sandcastles and race toy boats.

I walked along the beach and immersed myself in my memories. I remembered the smell of the saltwater and the feeling of the sand beneath my feet. I approached the water and felt the waves come to me and then retreat, like a hug.

As I walked back home, I saw a group of children playing at the shore. It reminded me of how fun it was to be young and play without worries. I smiled as I watched them and was glad to have had the opportunity to enjoy a day at the beach.

The waves of the sea reminded me that happy memories can be found anywhere. Although I may forget some things over time, I will always remember how beautiful that day at the beach was.

I will always be okay

Sometimes I worry about the future, but I always try to remember that I will be okay. I know that I have many people in my life who love me and take care of me. Even though I may feel confused or lost at times, I know that I am not alone.

I remember when I was a child, my grandmother used to sing me a song that said "I will always be okay, even when the storm is here." It made me feel better to know that, even though life can be tough at times, there will always be a light at the end of the tunnel.

Even though I sometimes feel a bit forgetful or disoriented, I know that there are things I can do to help myself feel better. I enjoy reading, walking, and doing crafts. These things help me relax and find peace.

I know that the future can be uncertain, but I have faith that everything will work out. I am grateful for all the good things in my life, and I know that there is always something to smile about.

So, no matter what happens, I will always be okay. I have hope that my happy memories and love for life will always be with me, and that I will continue to find beautiful things in the world around me.

The end.

Made in United States
North Haven, CT
20 April 2023